SPECIAL THANKS TO MICHAEL TAYLOR FOR
THE STEADY STREAM OF GREAT IDEAS!

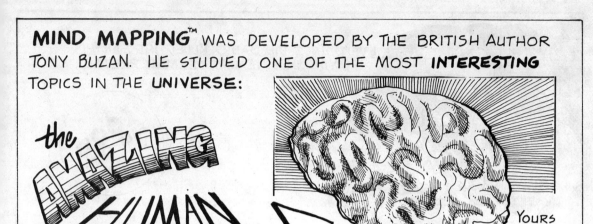

MIND MAPPING™ WAS DEVELOPED BY THE BRITISH AUTHOR TONY BUZAN. HE STUDIED ONE OF THE MOST **INTERESTING** TOPICS IN THE **UNIVERSE**:

the AMAZING HUMAN BRAIN

YOURS IS GROWING AND CHANGING AS YOU READ THIS!

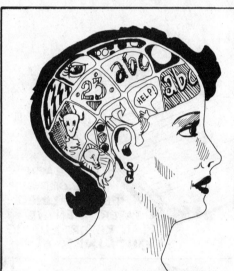

THERE IS A LOT WE DON'T KNOW ABOUT THE BRAIN.

WE **DO** KNOW THAT **EVERY BRAIN** HAS AT LEAST **TWO** DIFFERENT WAYS OF TAKING IN AND **PROCESSING** INFORMATION.

ONE WAY

THE "LOGICAL THINKING STYLE" HAS BEEN AROUND FOR A LONG TIME...

FOR MANY TASKS YOUR BRAIN IS QUITE HAPPY WITH WORDS IN SENTENCES LINED UP NEATLY ON A PAGE. IT LIKES THE ORDER OF AN OUTLINE, TOO.

YES!

HOWEVER, WHEN YOU WANT TO COME UP WITH CREATIVE NEW, IDEAS AND LOOK AT HOW IDEAS CONNECT WITH EACH OTHER, YOU NEED TO USE COLOR, PICTURES & SYMBOLS

AND THAT'S WHERE MIND MAPPING COMES IN!

THIS IS a drawing of a cross-section of the human brain, made by slicing the brain "from ear to ear."

DO NOT TRY THIS AT HOME.

darn.

MIND MAPS ARE MADE ON UNLINED PAPER, USING COLOR, SYMBOLS, PICTURES AND KEY WORDS.

SO, WHEN YOU MAKE MIND MAPS YOU WILL BE USING YOUR WHOLE BRAIN!

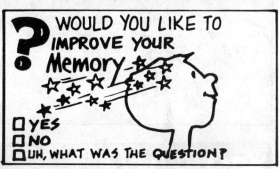

BEFORE YOU BEGIN MIND MAPPING, YOU NEED TO FEEL COMFORTABLE DRAWING SIMPLE PICTURES AND CARTOONS...

AT SOME TIME IN YOUR LIFE YOU PROBABLY **LOVED** TO DRAW.

BUT YOU MAY HAVE DEVELOPED AN INNER VOICE THAT SCREAMED...

YOU CAN'T DRAW!

THE FACT IS, **EVERYONE** CAN LEARN TO DRAW.

ALL IT TAKES IS **PRACTICE** AND AN OPEN MIND!

TAKE A GOOD LOOK AT THIS GUY.

HE'S MADE OF SIMPLE DOTS, LINES, AND CURVES:

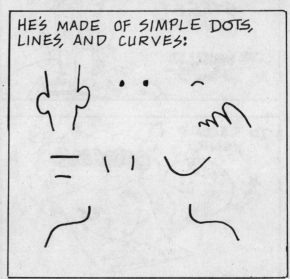

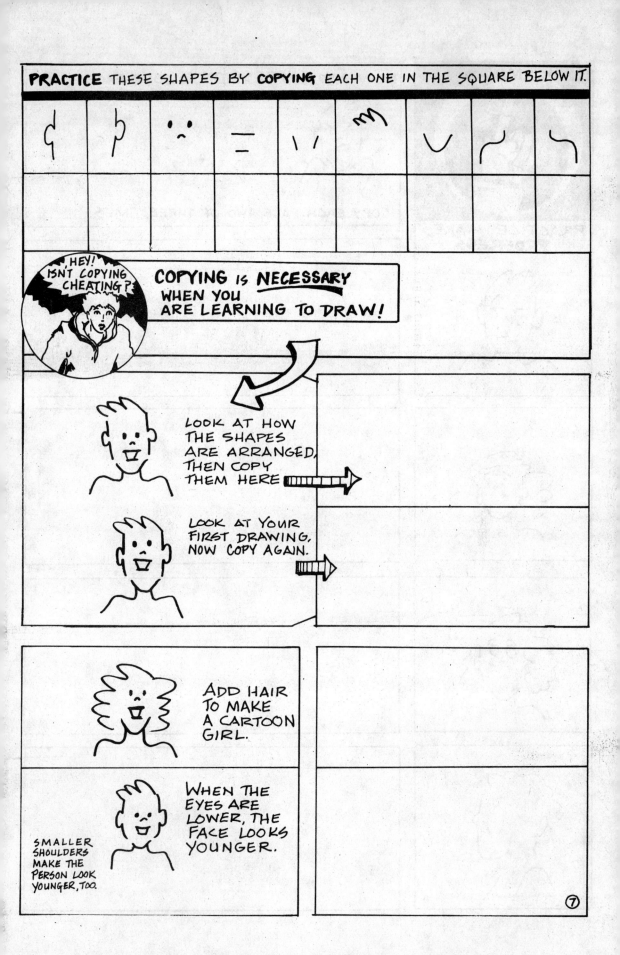

PRACTICE THESE SHAPES BY COPYING EACH ONE IN THE SQUARE BELOW IT.

HEY! ISN'T COPYING CHEATING?

COPYING IS NECESSARY WHEN YOU ARE LEARNING TO DRAW!

LOOK AT HOW THE SHAPES ARE ARRANGED, THEN COPY THEM HERE

LOOK AT YOUR FIRST DRAWING, NOW COPY AGAIN.

ADD HAIR TO MAKE A CARTOON GIRL.

WHEN THE EYES ARE LOWER, THE FACE LOOKS YOUNGER.

SMALLER SHOULDERS MAKE THE PERSON LOOK YOUNGER, TOO.

⑦

REMEMBER:

PRACTICE MAKES **PROGRESS**

NOW ADD EXPRESSION TO YOUR FACES:

COPY EACH FACE TWO OR THREE TIMES.

OF COURSE, DRAWINGS OF FACES CAN BE QUITE SIMPLE,

OR **VERY COMPLEX**...

AND EVERYTHING IN BETWEEN.

COPY SOME OF THESE FACES, THEN MAKE UP A FEW OF YOUR OWN.

THIS SPACE RESERVED FOR YOU! ☆

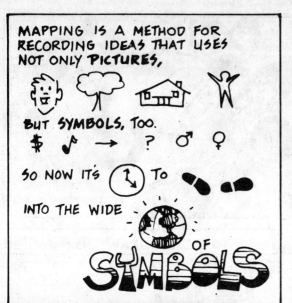

MAPPING IS A METHOD FOR RECORDING IDEAS THAT USES NOT ONLY **PICTURES**,

BUT SYMBOLS, TOO.

SO NOW IT'S TIME TO INTO THE WIDE

WHEN YOU USE SYMBOLS ON YOUR MIND MAPS, IT HELPS YOU TAKE NOTES **QUICKLY**

YOU CAN DRAW AN ENVELOPE FASTER THAN YOU CAN WRITE "LETTER."

YOU WILL DECIDE WHAT A SYMBOL MEANS FOR YOUR MAP. A CLOUD COULD BE

A THOUGHT

IMAGINATION

RAIN

TROUBLE

WITH PRACTICE, YOU WILL BE ABLE TO THINK OF SYMBOLS FOR MANY IDEAS.

GOOD IDEA

PICTURES AND SYMBOLS MAKE YOUR NOTES MORE **MEMORABLE**

REMEMBER

TRY COPYING EACH OF THESE USEFUL SYMBOLS:

  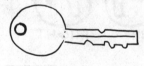

THESE SYMBOLS MIGHT COME IN HANDY LATER IN THIS COMIC...

DAVID ORCUTT IS THE INVENTOR OF **SYMBOLVISION**, A NEW LANGUAGE THAT CAN BE USED TO COMMUNICATE THROUGHOUT THE **WORLD**.

DAVID'S DREAM IS THAT SOMEDAY **EVERYONE ON EARTH** WILL BE ABLE TO UNDERSTAND EACH OTHER...

BY SIGNING WHEN THEY ARE FACE FACE TO FACE...

AND USING SYMBOLS TO COMMUNICATE ON PAPER AND COMPUTERS.

MANY OF THE SYMBOLS COLLECTED AND DEVELOPED BY DAVID ORCUTT AND THE WORLDSIGN COMMUNICATION SOCIETY ARE **GREAT** FOR MIND MAPPING...

TOWN

CITY

LEFT   RIGHT

GROW

KISS

MONTH

HOT or HEAT   COOK

ENERGY

LIFE

SUN

CRY

FUTURE   PAST   ALWAYS

MEET

BEND OR BOW

SOME OF THESE SYMBOLS LIKE ⚀ AND ⚛ ARE "BORROWED" OTHERS ARE BRAND **NEW.**

More Symbolvision:

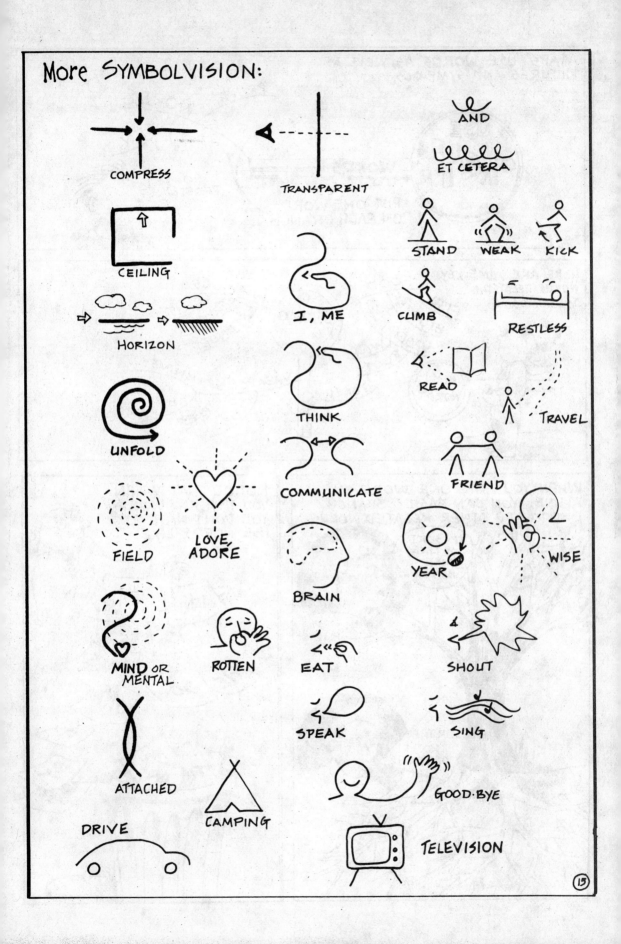

COMPRESS

TRANSPARENT

AND

ET CETERA

CEILING

HORIZON

I, ME

THINK

UNFOLD

FIELD

LOVE, ADORE

COMMUNICATE

BRAIN

MIND OR MENTAL

ROTTEN

EAT

SHOUT

SPEAK

SING

ATTACHED

CAMPING

DRIVE

TELEVISION

STAND   WEAK   KICK

CLIMB

RESTLESS

READ

TRAVEL

FRIEND

YEAR

WISE

GOOD·BYE

MAPS USE **WORDS** AS WELL AS PICTURES AND SYMBOLS.

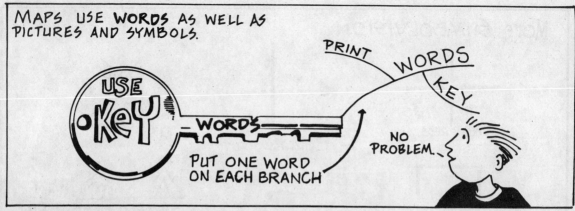

HERE ARE SOME KEY WORDS RELATED TO ESKIMOS.

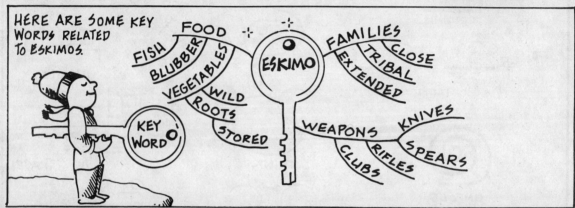

WHEN YOU PRINT ONE WORD ON A LINE, YOU CAN EASILY BRANCH OUT TO ADD OTHER RELATED WORDS.

NOTICE THAT WHEN YOU USE **KEY WORDS** YOU DON'T HAVE TO USE WORDS LIKE

EXTENSIVE GLOBAL RESEARCH INDICATES THAT MOST PEOPLE CAN'T READ THEIR **OWN NOTES.**

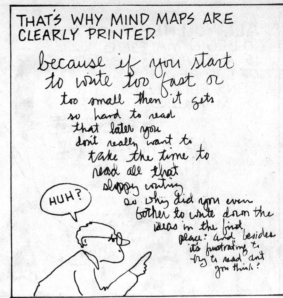

THAT'S WHY MIND MAPS ARE CLEARLY PRINTED.

because if you start to write too fast or too small then it gets so hard to read that later you don't really want to take the time to read all that sloppy writing so why did you even bother to write down the ideas in the first place? and besides its frustrating to try to read ain't you think?

YOUR PRINTING WILL IMPROVE IF YOU PRACTICE THESE BASICS:

IIIIIITTT OOOOOCCCRRR SSSS

NOW COPY ABCDEGHJKMNOPRSUVXY

THE TIME FOR PRACTICE IS NOW. TAKE YOUR TIME.

A

B

C

R

NOW WRITE YOUR OWN SENTENCES BELOW ↓

ALL YOU NEED TO BEGIN MAPPING IS A HANDFUL OF COLORED PENS, PENCILS OR MARKERS...

THIS COMIC AND A *TOPIC*.

THE TOPIC FOR YOUR FIRST PRACTICE MAP IS:

MY IDEAL FUTURE

IMAGINE THAT YOU HAVE A **MAGIC WAND** AND CAN CREATE **ANY** FUTURE YOU WISH!

BEGIN YOUR MAP WITH A CENTRAL IMAGE. USE A PICTURE OR SYMBOL...

MAYBE A CALENDAR, A CRYSTAL BALL OR A **MAGIC WAND**.

YOU MIGHT WANT TO ADD A NUMBER OR DATE TO REPRESENT ONE YEAR FROM NOW, FIVE YEARS FROM NOW, OR MORE.

AFTER YOU DRAW A SYMBOL IN THE CENTER OF THE PAGE, **RELAX** AND LET THE IDEAS COME TO YOU.

RECORD EACH IDEA

USING A KEY WORD OR SYMBOL.

BRANCH OUT FROM THERE.

YOUR MAP WILL **GROW** AS YOU ADD NEW IDEAS.

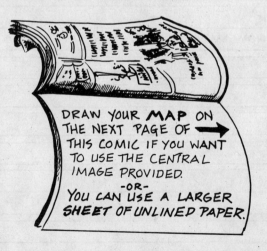

DRAW YOUR **MAP** ON THE NEXT PAGE OF THIS COMIC IF YOU WANT TO USE THE CENTRAL IMAGE PROVIDED. —OR— YOU CAN USE A LARGER **SHEET** OF UNLINED PAPER.

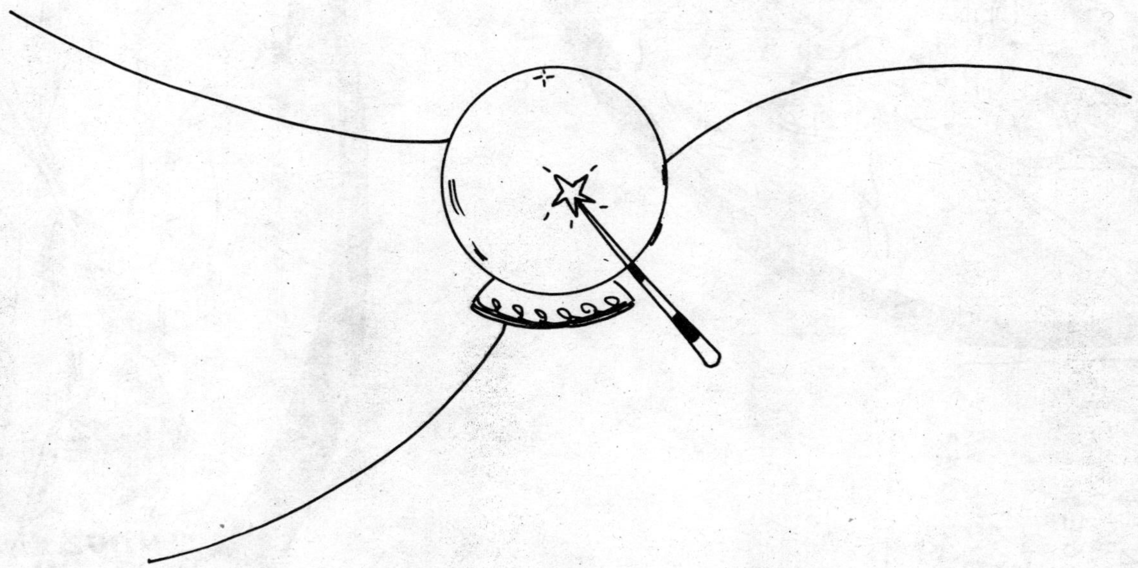

PRACTICE MAP 1

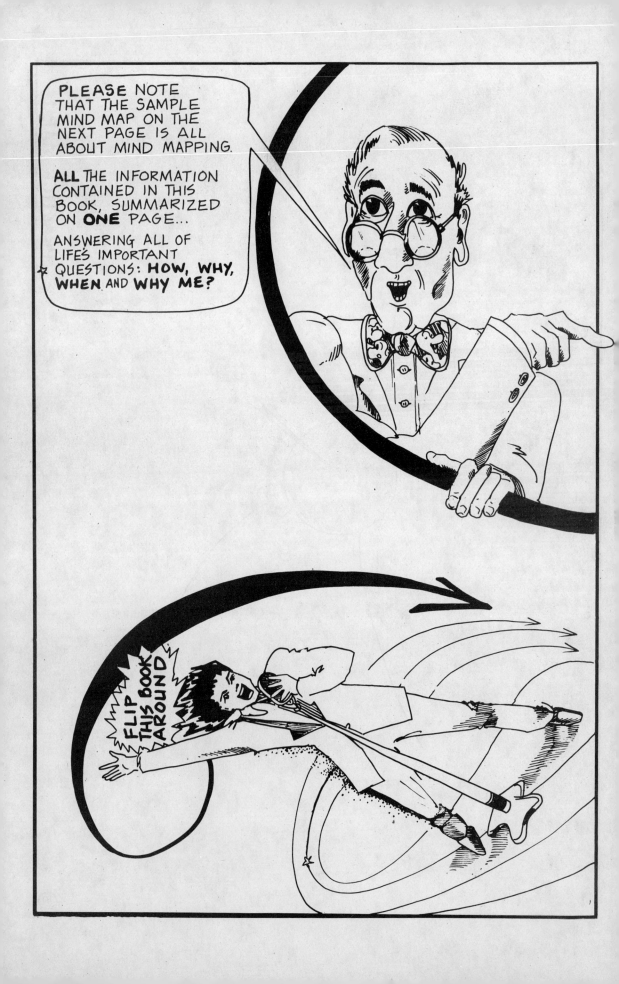

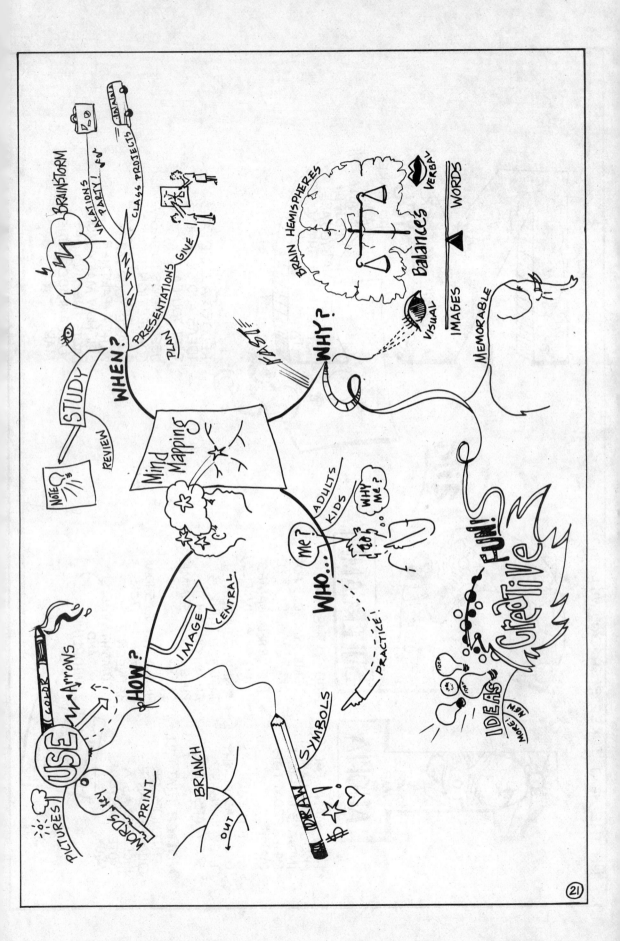

Subject? Study?

A BLANK PAGE FOR **YOU** TO MAKE A MAP ON ANY SUBJECT THAT YOU ARE STUDYING RIGHT NOW (PAGE 25)

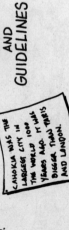

- RECORD ALL THE FACTS, IDEAS AND QUESTIONS THAT YOU CAN.

- USE ARROWS TO SHOW CONNECTIONS

- SHARE YOUR MAP WITH A PARTNER. SEE HOW MANY MORE FACTS THE TWO OF YOU CAN ADD TO THE MAP.

and

A MAP ABOUT **SUPERCAMP**

A SAMPLE MAP ON **CAHOKIA**

- HOW MANY FACTS ABOUT THE CAHOKIA INDIANS CAN YOU READ FROM THIS MAP?

- WHAT IS YOUR GUESS AS TO WHY THEY VANISHED 500 YEARS AGO?

NOTICE THAT FULL SENTENCES OR QUOTES CAN BE INCLUDED AS A "NOTE" ON YOUR MAPS.

- **ADD** TO THE MAP:
  → SOME SYMBOLS FOR SPORTS
  → THE WORD "GAMES" (PART OF ACTIVITIES)
  → A NEW GUIDELINE THAT YOU THINK IS AN IMPORTANT RULE FOR A SUMMER CAMP.
  → FIND A WAY TO SHOW THE CONNECTION BETWEEN COMMITMENT AND GUIDELINES

CAHOKIA WAS THE LARGEST CITY IN THE WORLD 1000 YEARS AGO. IT WAS BIGGER THAN PARIS AND LONDON.

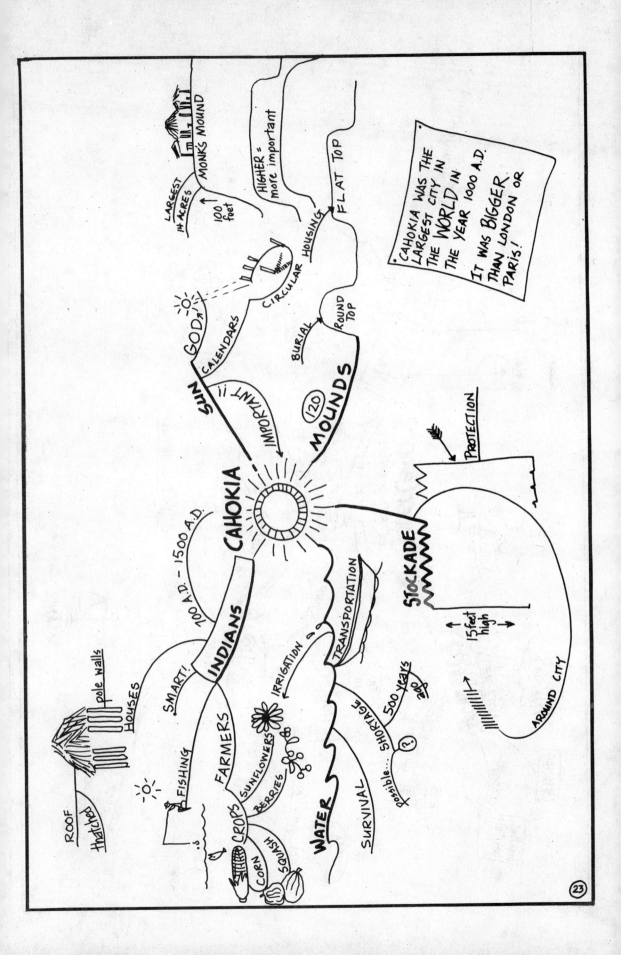

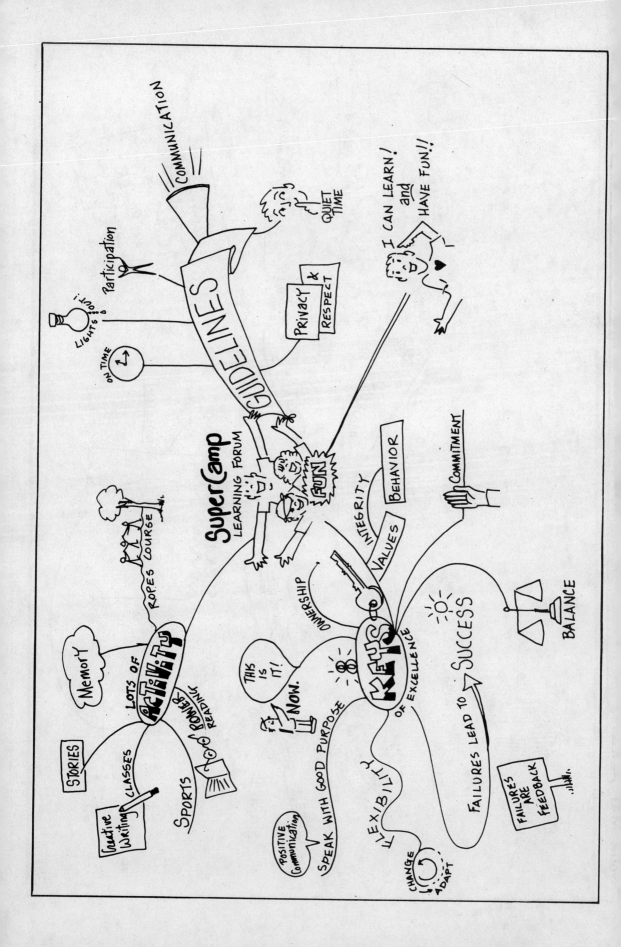

YOU CAN **STUDY** USING MINDSCAPES. YOU CAN TAKE NOTES,
REVIEW FOR TESTS OR PREPARE A **BOOK REPORT.**
HERE ARE A FEW MINDSCAPE IDEAS FOR BOOK REPORTS:

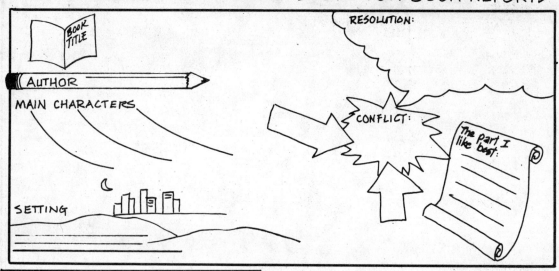

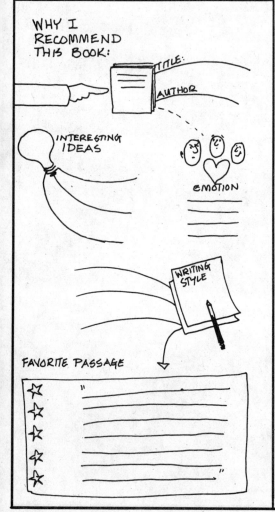

YOUR MINDSCAPE HERE... RECORD IDEAS AND THOUGHTS ABOUT A FAVORITE BOOK...

NOW REMEMBER, FOLLOW THE RULES OF MIND MAPPING AND PRACTICE, PRACTICE PRACTICE!

- BEGIN WITH A CENTRAL IMAGE
- PUT ONE WORD ON EACH BRANCH.
- USE KEY WORDS, SYMBOLS, PICTURES AND CARTOONS
- CONTINUE TO BRANCH OUT AS YOU ADD NEW IDEAS TO THE MAP.

PRACTICE MAKES PROGRESS.

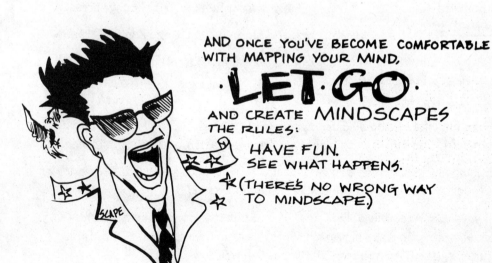

AND ONCE YOU'VE BECOME COMFORTABLE WITH MAPPING YOUR MIND,

·LET·GO·

AND CREATE MINDSCAPES
THE RULES:

HAVE FUN.
SEE WHAT HAPPENS.

☆ (THERE'S NO WRONG WAY TO MINDSCAPE.)

RESOURCES

Brookes, Mona. 1986. *Drawing with Children.* Los Angeles: J.P. Tarcher.

———. 1991. *Drawing for Older Children and Teens.* Los Angeles: J.P. Tarcher.

DePorter, Bobbie. 1992. *Quantum Learning.* New York: Dell.

———. 1994. *Unleashing the Genius within You.* Oceanside, Calif.: Learning Forum.

Edwards, Betty. 1979. *Drawing on the Right Side of the Brain.* Los Angeles: J.P. Tarcher.

Gautier, Dick. 1989. *The Creative Cartoonist.* New York: Putnam.

———. 1993. *Drawing and Cartooning 1,001 Faces.* New York: Putnam.

Jensen, Eric. 1988. *Super-Teaching.* Del Mar, Calif.: Turning Point.

Margulies, Nancy. 1991. *Mapping Inner Space.* Tucson, Ariz.: Zephyr Press.

———. 1993. *Maps, Mindscapes, and More.* Tucson, Ariz.: Zephyr Press.

Tatchell, Judy. 1988. *How to Draw Cartoons, Monsters, Animals, and Machines.* London: Usborne.

For more information on SuperCamp call 1-800-228-LEARN. SuperCamp promises "Ten fun days to higher grades, motivation, and self-confidence."

Symbolvision materials can be obtained by writing to David Orcutt, Worldsign Exposition, Perry Siding, Winlaw, B.C. Canada, V0G2J0.

If you live in Australia, Glen Capelli is one expert in your country on creativity and learning. Contact him at the True Learning Centre, PO Box 176, South Perth, Western Australia 6151. Phone 474-1752.